# PRAISE ABOUT THE AUTHOR

"Tanya has a calm spiritual presence and an amazing array of tactical tools and skills. This gives her a tremendous ability to connect at a deep, personal level while guiding you through doing exactly what it takes to find your success. I recommend Tanya for anyone looking to grow personally or deepen your teams' relationships."

**- BRAD EDWARDS**
*Experience Designer*

"Something amazing happens when you sit across the table from someone who is the real deal. Their words have gravity because you know they are true. This is what it feels like to learn from, and be coached by, Tanya Unterbrunner. She isn't a coach who simply wants to have coffee and talk about your problems. She's the coach who is going to dissect where you're at, and why. Then carve out a path to real growth. If you want to slay your giants, you want Tanya involved."

- **JORDAN LOFTIS**
*Author of The Men With Bare Feet and Speaker*

"Tanya has earned my highest recommendations as an executive coach. She has a unique ability to recognize and understand the challenges of business professionals. Tanya creates a culture in her coaching approach to tactfully challenge her clients, while holding them accountable to their goals and objectives. She is able to ask the right questions to create an environment of looking at situations as opportunities for success."

**- ROBIN WEIBENGA**
*Consultant*

"Tanya has a true gift for connecting with and relating to people of all walks of life. As a coach and teacher, like a ray of sunshine, she is able to help people identify their important goals and gently guide them toward a successful future. I would recommend Tanya for anyone looking to find greater happiness, purpose, and meaning in their lives."

**- DR. MIKE ELLIOT**
*MD | SVPMA & CMO*
*Avera McKennan Hospital & University Health Center*

# Catapult

TANYA UNTERBRUNNER

# Catapult

TOOLS HIGH ACHIEVERS USE TO CREATE SUCCESS IN ALL AREAS OF THEIR LIVES

Copyright 2018 © By Tanya Unterbrunner

ISBN: 978-1-949550-02-3

Ebook ISBN: 978-1-949550-03-0

All rights reserved. No part of this book may be reproduced or transmitted in any form or by any means, electronic or mechanical, including photocopying, recording or by any information storage and retrieval system, without permission in writing from the copyright owner. For information on distribution rights, royalties, derivative works or licensing opportunities on behalf of this content or work, please contact the publisher at the address below.

Printed in the United States of America.

Lead Design: Amy Gehling

Publishing Manager: Brooke Brown

Although the author and publisher have made every effort to ensure that the information and advice in this book was correct and accurate at press time, the author and publisher do not assume and hereby disclaim any liability to any party for any loss, damage, or disruption caused from acting upon the information in this book or by errors or omissions, whether such errors or omissions result from negligence, accident, or any other cause.

Throne Publishing Group

2329 N. Career Ave. #241

Sioux Falls, SD 57107

www.ThronePG.com

# Dedication

I dedicate this book to every single person I have ever encountered, for they have helped shape me into who I am today. My family, friends, and clients who have supported me along the way have oftentimes seen things in me that I was unable to see within myself. Some of my biggest lessons were learned through the toughest struggles, and God, along with all my guardian angels, have all helped me learn the lessons with as much grace as possible. To all of you, thank you and I love you.

# Table of Contents

**CHAPTER ONE** — 2
*The Unfair Advantage*

**CHAPTER TWO** — 24
*The Wheel*

**CHAPTER THREE** — 42
*Finding Time*

**CHAPTER FOUR** — 62
*Prove It! (Show Me)*

**CHAPTER FIVE** — 80
*Make The Vision - Make It Real*

**CHAPTER SIX** — 100
*Your Life Purpose*

**CHAPTER SEVEN** — 120
*Your Choice*

**ABOUT THE AUTHOR** — 138

**ABOUT THE COMPANY** — 144

# Chapter One

**THE UNFAIR ADVANTAGE**

# Chapter One

## THE UNFAIR ADVANTAGE

In your mind, picture an Olympic athlete. What skills do they have? Are they competing at a high level and succeeding? Now, ask yourself, what does it take for them to succeed? Most often, I think we'll come up with an answer about their skill, strength, or speed, but often we don't consider the people who are behind their success. Olympic athletes are incredibly gifted, but their God-given abilities can only take them so far. It takes a coach to show them how to use their abilities to perform at their highest level. A coach can show an Olympian how to maximize their potential and achieve success by honing their skills and giving them clear guidance. The same is true in our lives, but many people fail to see the importance of a coach in their ordinary, daily lives.

Those who've never truly experienced transformational guidance from a professional life coach might question its purpose and how it can bring real value to their lives. Oftentimes, people fail to see how life coaching can benefit them, as they focus on singular aspects of their lives. When we are too focused on one part of our lives instead of seeing multiple dimensions working together, we're not as successful as we could be.

Many people struggle to see the whole picture of their lives, and, therefore, often fail to recognize how each aspect will affect the others. Coaches are able to clearly perceive the whole reality—the big picture. We focus on all areas of a person's life, because each aspect has a significant impact on everything else. Our total life has an impact on business, relationships, and everything else, because everywhere we go, we take our whole selves with us.

As a coach, I can bring real value to your business and each part of your life by guiding you toward transformation of your whole self. We are better able to perform and live well if our lives are balanced and healthy. The goal of the kind of coaching I do is to equip people with the skills and knowledge needed to succeed in all areas of their lives. Quality coaching produces lasting change, and I can help you transform your life.

Coaching is for anyone who wants to move forward in life, to take the bull by the horns and go. It is about wise, fast action steps. Coaching helps people distinguish where they are in life, and where they want to be. It creates action steps to get there in the fastest, most successful way possible.

## MENTORING AND CONSULTING

There are other ways to gain knowledge and guidance that will help us succeed. Coaching is often confused for other helpful relationships, such as mentoring, consulting, and counseling. While these other relationships can add value to our lives, they either focus on a specific area of our life, or they are more retrospective and less forward-thinking.

Mentoring and consulting tend to look more specifically at a particular industry or area of life. When looking for a mentor, we typically look for someone who has had success with whichever part of our lives we are seeking guidance in. They can help us succeed by teaching us the knowledge and skills that helped them succeed. In a mentoring relationship, we are often in their business shadowing them. Consulting is similar, but a consultant is focused directly on our business and has a direct impact while steering us in the right direction. A consultant is also a person who has been successful in our industry, and they guide us toward success.

## COUNSELING

Counseling is a very different relationship. It helps us gain clarity on why we have arrived at a particular place in our lives. A counselor is someone who can help us understand ourselves, based off of where we have come from. Counselors are helpful when we need a greater understanding of ourselves and, possibly, our past, which can be very valuable.

## LIFE COACHING

Life coaching and counseling are similar, but there are some very distinct lines between the two. Counselors are able to take a deep dive, diagnose mental instabilities, articulate the cause and effect of past behaviors, and help us see who we truly are. Life coaches may look at where we are now, but are primarily concerned with the future and how we can become the best versions of ourselves.

Life coaching is also diverse, as it focuses on a person's entire life. There are specialized, or niche, types of coaching, such as executive, finance, and health and wellness coaching. Executive coaches are like consultants or mentors that help executives perform better at work. Financial coaches offer guidance to help people handle their finances responsibly. And health and wellness coaches work with people who would like to be physically healthier. While niche coaching is important and can benefit people's lives, transformational life coaching focuses on all of those aspects of life simultaneously, with the goal of catapulting each person toward success.

## CATAPULT COACHING

Looking back on my experience as a coach, I've realized there needs to be a change in the way coaching is done. Too often, coaches help their clients feel good, but don't help them find transformation that makes a lasting change in their lives. Coaching needs to be about improving the lives of clients, helping them distinguish action-based steps to achieve success and lead more fulfilled lives. There needs to be an emphasis on depth in coaching, otherwise it will only improve people's lives on a surface level, rather than providing significant change. This is where Catapult Coaching comes in.

Catapult Coaching is a comprehensive, transformational process. Catapult Coaching is a thoughtful examination of each aspect of your life, and how you can grow in each area to reach your desired level of success. Based on action-based goals that will motivate you to grow in each area of your life, Catapult Coaching is an empowering redirection of your life that will CATAPULT you toward the life you want to live.

If you want to go deeper, take action-based steps toward success, and have results, transformation, and growth in your life, then you are ready to be coached. Although typical life coaching covers many aspects of your life, Catapult Coaching goes deeper. While many of my clients come to me wanting a specific change in their life, such as a promotion or to retire early, I go deeper with them, looking at all of the aspects of their life, and what they can do to become a better whole person and live successfully. At the end of our coaching relationship, they will have the confidence to tackle any goal, or any challenge for that matter, head on. I help them become healthier people who are more capable of achieving success and living well. As your Catapult coach, I will do the same.

Catapult Coaching begins with looking at every part of your life and finding the common cause of strife or disfunction. There is typically a root cause or common denominator that causes pain or issues in our lives. Through Catapult Coaching, I can look into your life and get to the core of what needs to change for you to transform and grow toward success.

My coaching is not symptomatic treatment. I won't give you an aspirin for your headache or give you a bandaid for your issues. Transformation and success begin with recognizing the root of what is holding you back. You might think you can do that on your own, but you would really be doing a disservice to yourself. We often fail to see the whole pictures of our lives, because it is hard to honestly confront our problems and recognize our struggles. I have a phrase that sums this up: self doesn't help. It takes the unbiased, insightful perspective of someone trained to identify the various aspects and crippling problems in your life to begin the process toward transformation. Through looking at the whole picture of your life, I can look to the core of your problems and catapult your struggles into success.

I believe in Catapult Coaching because I have seen it transform people's lives. I am passionate about coaching people to become the best versions of themselves and helping them live fuller, richer lives. You may have heard of coaching before, and you might have a preconceived notion about it, but I have extensive experience as a coach and education to back it up. I have a Bachelor of Science degree in Psychology: Life Coaching, and I have certificates from the American Association of Christian Counselors in a variety of professional coaching specializations, including Addictions and Recovery, Executive, Leadership and Organizational, Health and Wellness, Christian, Financial, and Marriage and Family.

Throughout my life and my work as a coach, I have seen and experienced a wide spectrum of circumstances. I have gone through times of triumph, and I also have experiences with death and loss. Those personal experiences have given me the insight needed to help clients navigate similar circumstances. Through it all, I have been fortunate enough to learn how to equip others to conquer their challenges and grow toward success and a fulfilling life. I am equipped to help others look into their lives, and give them clear direction that isn't biased by emotion. I'm not afraid to take on challenges and have difficult conversations. I can identify what you need, and I can be the voice of reason and direction. And, as I have done in my life, I can give you action-based goals to pursue that will transform your life.

If you recognize you are struggling in certain areas of your life, or you feel as though you aren't living up to your potential, now might be the time to change it all. This is about turning your struggles into success, by identifying the root cause of your troubles and creating action-based goals to help you grow, transform, and play your game at a higher level. If you are ready to pursue your purpose and live a more fulfilling life, to achieve success in the quickest, best way possible, then my coaching service, Catapult Coaching, is for you.

In this book you'll find some tools that will help you achieve success, but remember, self doesn't help. Ultimately, you need the unbiased, clear, direct guidance of a Catapult Coach. If you use the tools in this book, you will certainly see a change in your life. If you want to achieve the fullness of transformation and success, hire a coach to guide you!

# JOURNAL, SKETCH, BRAINSTORM

CHAPTER ONE: THE UNFAIR ADVANTAGE

# Chapter Two

## THE WHEEL

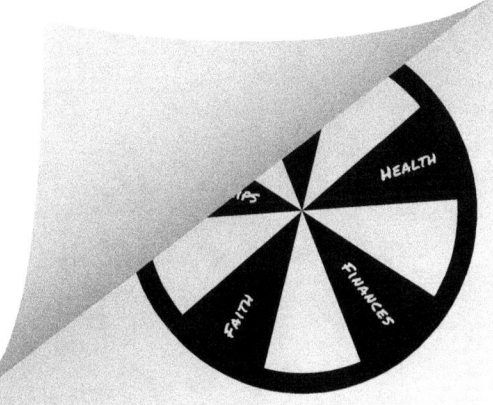

# Chapter Two

## THE WHEEL

I first learned about "The Wheel" early on in my career as a coach. I was in a Coach Mastermind Group where I learned new tools and techniques from other coaches. At that time, not many people in my area knew what coaching really was, so I worked with most of my clients online or over the phone. When I saw the value that "The Wheel" could bring them, I really wanted to share that tool with my clients. Though it was difficult, I did my best to vocally describe the tool and give directions that would optimize its helpfulness. In turn, that really allowed me to change it up a little and use it in a way that best served my clients.

One of my early successes with helping a client use the wheel was with a client who was dealing with a lot of social anxiety and fear. I described "The Wheel" to her over the phone, and we began looking at all of the different aspects of her life. Through looking at her life with "The Wheel" in mind,

I was able to show her where she was off balance. Rather than focusing only on her fear, she had a clearer picture of her whole life. It brought everything into perspective and diminished her fear. She loved this tool and used it on a weekly basis to make sure her life was as balanced as possible.

Throughout my career as a coach, I've seen "The Wheel" give many people a new level of self-awareness that sets them on the path to transformation. Over and over again, I've seen clients gain a clearer view of their lives just by using this tool. It is an essential tool for growth, because transformation begins with a realistic perspective.

"The Wheel" is a tool that helps you visualize all of the parts of your life. The parts I focus on are career, relationships, faith, finances, and health. Each aspect is like a spoke on a wheel. In order to have a well-balanced wheel that is capable of rolling smoothly, each spoke has to be even in length. Too often, though, some of our spokes are longer or shorter than the others. If we are overly focused on work and it is taking up more time in our lives than is healthy, our work spoke will be much longer than others. Our lives can become unbalanced if we are giving too much or too little attention to any part, and then our wheels won't roll smoothly. Our wheel will be wobbly if the spokes aren't even, which will cause disruption in our lives and hold us back from success.

Transformation begins with a realistic perspective of your life. Visualizing your life like a wheel is a good place to start, because it will show you where you're off balance. When you are able to see which of your spokes are uneven, you'll know where you need to improve. It gives you an overview of your life and you'll have a realistic visual of where you're at. When you have a clear perspective of your life, there is typically something unbalanced that is screaming out at you that needs attention. Most of us have uneven wheels; we focus too much on one part of our lives and not enough on others. "The Wheel" helps you identify how you need to shift your focus, which is necessary for growth. If you are unbalanced in your life, you won't be able to perform well. Just as a wheel with uneven spokes can't roll smoothly, you can't live into your full potential if your life is unbalanced.

Growing into your full potential begins with balancing all aspects of your life. Highly successful people use "The Wheel" on a regular basis, because their success comes from living balanced lives. They are able to perform at a high level because their lives run smoothly like an even wheel. I've seen "The Wheel" work hundreds of times for my clients, making their lives more balanced and bringing them closer to success. However, you might not know what steps to take to become more balanced. You'll need help from someone else, because self doesn't help.

A coach is able to help you pinpoint which parts of your life are uneven. More than that, though, they'll help you create action-based steps to balance each aspect of your life. If you're struggling in your work, marriage, or another part of your life, the spokes on your wheel are most likely uneven. Using "The Wheel", especially with the guidance of a coach, will give you a realistic perspective of your life. It's a reality check that can catapult you toward transformation. When you realize how unbalanced your life is, you'll recognize your need for change. You'll hunger for growth. Working with a coach will ensure you don't slip back into an unbalanced lifestyle. Self doesn't help; transformation comes from a realistic perspective of your current situation and insightful guidance that will lead you toward your goal. A coach is a voice of reason who can show you how to become balanced, which will cause a significant amount of growth and transformation in your life.

If you recognize that parts of your life are uneven and you want to grow and achieve success, you need to make a change. Successful people's lives run smoothly because they realize a successful life begins with being a healthy, balanced person. You can't operate at the highest level in any part of your life if you are giving too much attention to one thing, such as work. As your coach, I can show you which parts of your wheel are uneven, what you need to do to make your wheel turn smoothly, and how to live a balanced life that will CATAPULT you toward success. If you feel motivated to make a change right now, contact me and I'll help you begin to significantly improve your life. Otherwise, visualize your life as a wheel, consider what changes need to be made for your life to be balanced, and read the next chapter to learn about another tool that will positively impact your life.

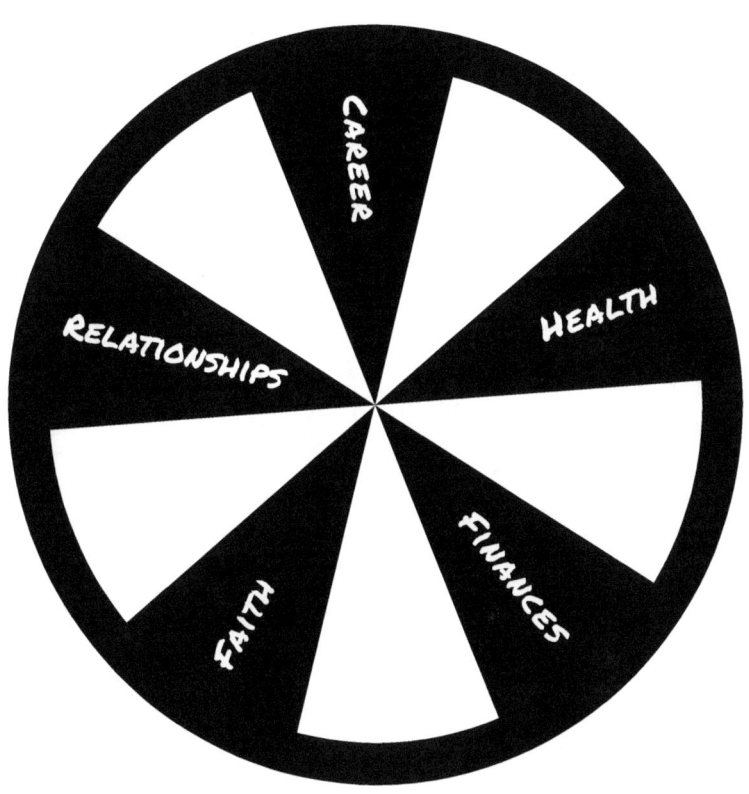

# Journal, Sketch, Brainstorm

CHAPTER TWO: THE WHEEL

CHAPTER TWO: THE WHEEL

CHAPTER TWO: THE WHEEL

CHAPTER TWO: THE WHEEL

# Chapter Three

**FINDING TIME**

# Chapter Three

## FINDING TIME

When I was sixteen my life changed dramatically. I became a teen mom and took on a load of responsibilities most teens don't have to handle. I learned to adapt and take on my new circumstances like an adult. I took it upon myself to find success in my new situation, with the hope of showing other teen moms they could do it, too.

I continued going to school, I lived in my own apartment with a baby, I worked two jobs, continued high school, and I had to adapt to new circumstances. I tried to balance life as a new mother, a student, and a teenager who wanted to have fun, but it wasn't easy. I was determined to make the best of my situation, but I started to have panic and anxiety attacks because I felt so overwhelmed.

Fortunately, I had enough insight to look for a way to relax and balance things in my life. There were lots of things I had to do, and there were things I wanted to do. I was stressed out by feeling like there wasn't enough time to do both, so I realized I needed to find the time. I began to look closely at my schedule. I had an academic planner and my personal calendar that gave me an outline of all my responsibilities. I took a hard look at what I absolutely needed to accomplish every day, and I considered what I wanted to do. I wanted to incorporate fun things, such as spending time with my friends, into my schedule. I found a way to make time for it all, even though my daily schedule was full.

A typical day for me when I was sixteen was filled to the brim with responsibilities. If there was anyone who could have said they didn't have time, it was me. I was up in the middle of the night because my son had his nights and days switched around. I would do my homework until he fell asleep again. Then I would wake up around six, and the first thing I would do was look at my schedule to figure out where I needed to be that day. I would go through the details of my day and visualize how I was going to accomplish everything while I was getting ready. There were a couple daycare options I used for my son, so my daily schedule depended on where I needed to take him. Often, I would take him to school with me because there was a daycare there. Then I would go to class, and, because of my academic success, I was able to leave school around lunchtime for the day. After class, I would either leave my son at the daycare at my school, or I would drop him off at another daycare. Then I would go to work for a couple hours, and after that I would go to another job until midnight. The next day would be about the same. I got an average of four hours of sleep every night, and I followed that schedule for two and a half years.

My life was busy and I had a lot of responsibilities as a teenager, but I didn't know there was any other way for me to live. I didn't think about how much I was taking on. I just did what I had to do. Since I was a teen mom, there were a lot of statistics that showed my life was over and I wasn't going to amount to anything. I felt a lot of responsibility to prove the statistics wrong, though, and I was conscious of people watching me. There were other teens who were going through similar circumstances, so I felt like I needed to show them that they could still be OK. I wanted to show them and others that there's a way to overcome unexpected situations in a healthy way. Hard stuff doesn't have to hold you back, and you don't have to be limited by a busy schedule. I used to feel held back by how much I had to do, but I found a way to make time for everything I had to accomplish and wanted to do.

I was able to handle a hectic slate of responsibilities with limited stress for two and a half years by looking carefully at my daily and weekly schedules. Once I had my priorities scheduled, I was able to plug in things I wanted to do when I had free time. Rather than feeling like I didn't have time because I was stressed, looking closely at my schedule gave me a realistic view of how much time I had each day. Even though my life was busy with new-found responsibilities, I was able to find the time to accomplish my tasks and enjoy myself. It wasn't easy to do, and I had to trade off some sleep sometimes, but I didn't feel limited or held back by my schedule. I was free to do everything I needed and wanted to do. I had every reason to feel stressed out and crushed by all of my responsibilities, but I didn't let that happen.

Unexpected things happen in our lives, but it's up to us to handle them in a healthy way. Instead of letting myself be held back by my circumstances, I used them to catapult me forward. By taking charge of my schedule, I was able to find the time not only to survive and do the bare minimum to get by, I was able to thrive and catapult myself and my family toward success.

Time is one of our most precious resources, but many people feel limited by it. It's not uncommon to feel overwhelmed by everything we have to accomplish in a day or week. You don't have to feel that way, though. Each of us has more time than we think. Time is the currency everyone has the same amount of, so it's up to you to use your time efficiently.

I was able to manage all of my responsibilities and accomplish my priorities when I was sixteen because I used my time efficiently. I took a realistic look at my schedule and set time for what I had to do and what I wanted to do. Even though I had a lot of responsibilities, I was able to find the time to accomplish everything and balance each aspect of my life, and you can, too.

Creating a detailed schedule is the first step to feeling like you have more freedom and time in your life. Begin by going through your week and writing down everything you did each day and how long it took. Be real and honest about what you spent your time doing each day. There are certain things you have to accomplish, such as work and family responsibilities. There are other things, though, that you want to accomplish because they are priorities to you. Once you have a daily list of what you spend time doing, consider how much time you realistically have to spend on responsibilities. Block off time in your daily and weekly schedule for everything you have to do, and then put that into a monthly calendar.

When you make a monthly calendar, you'll realize how much time you actually have to spend on other things you want to do, such as spending time with family or exercising. Ask yourself what your priorities are, and make time for them each week. If your health is a priority, make time for it in your schedule. You'll be able to live a more balanced life when you're able to accomplish your responsibilities and make time for your priorities.

When you efficiently schedule your time and accomplish everything you want to do and need to do, your life will become more balanced and fulfilling. You'll feel empowered and in control of your time, instead of feeling stressed out by everything you need to accomplish. Living a successful, fulfilling life happens when we take care of our responsibilities and have the freedom to pursue what's important to us. Successful people balance their responsibilities and priorities, making time for each and recognizing the importance of both. As you balance your life, it's important to use "The Wheel" to check how you're doing moving forward. "The Wheel" will help you determine if you're using more time than necessary for responsibilities, instead of balancing them with your priorities.

Once you find the time in your life to accomplish everything you need and want to do, you need to put your schedule into practice. We often have a habit of slipping back into an unhealthy or unproductive schedule, which prevents us from fulfilling our responsibilities or priorities. Just like a budget, your time is a resource you'll have to balance. There are some things you'll have to cut out of your monthly budget of time. You have to make a choice, though, to manage the responsibilities and priorities in your life, like I did as a teen mom, to live a healthier, more successful, and balanced life.

# JOURNAL, SKETCH, BRAINSTORM

CHAPTER THREE: FINDING TIME

CHAPTER THREE: FINDING TIME

# Chapter Four

**PROVE IT! (SHOW ME)**

# Chapter Four

## PROVE IT! (SHOW ME)

When I was in school studying psychology, I learned the technique of cognitive behavioral therapy (CBT). CBT is a technique that aims to change the way you feel by changing the way you think. It's a helpful tool that therapists use, and I was intrigued by it because I was able to use it on myself where I was struggling.

At that time, I was starting a coaching business, but I had a deep negative belief that I could never make it happen, and that I needed to have a traditional job to pay my bills. I had a passion for coaching and a strong desire to start a coaching business, but my passion and desire was held back by how I felt about myself. I knew God was calling me to start a coaching business, but I had negative core beliefs about myself that held me back from pursuing that calling. As I struggled with those negative thoughts, I used the CBT technique that I learned in school to investigate why I felt the way I did.

As I used CBT, I discovered the root of my struggles, the chain of negative beliefs and lies that were preventing me from living out my calling. I looked back on my life and reflected on the reason I thought negatively about myself. I was in an abusive relationship for ten very formative years. During that time, my boyfriend would tell me negative things such as I wasn't going to amount to anything and I was worthless. When I heard that from him, I was motivated to prove him wrong. I thought I had used his words purely as motivation, but it wasn't until I used CBT on myself that I realized they had stuck with me and shaped my negative core beliefs. Even though it had been years since I heard those words from him, they crept back into my life and held me back from pursuing my calling.

I knew I had to follow my calling to start a coaching business, so I had to free myself from being held back by my negative core beliefs. It began with using CBT to learn what my negative core beliefs were. Whenever I felt like my business wouldn't be successful, I would hold that negative emotion and explore it. Then I would ask myself, what was my thought immediately before that feeling?

Negative emotions are thought-induced, or linked to a voice within us that speaks negative beliefs, so I would investigate what thoughts were connected to my negative emotions. I discovered my negative emotions were induced by lies I believed about myself, such as the one my boyfriend used to tell me, that

I wouldn't amount to anything. I found that when I felt like I shouldn't start my coaching business, I was believing lies about myself that held me back. The problem was that they didn't feel like lies! They were my normal, and so they felt like my truths. I went through the surface level emotions, captured my thoughts, and got to the core negative belief, which was that I couldn't do it and I wasn't worth it.

When I got to the core of my negative beliefs, I didn't experience a dramatic transformation that set me free to pursue my calling. I had a greater understanding of myself, but that didn't make the lies go away. I held onto the lie that I wasn't going to amount to anything, that I couldn't do it, and I wasn't worth it, and I believed that about myself deep down. In order to follow my passion and desire and God's calling for my life, I had to change the lies I believed about myself into more positive truths. Each lie we believe about ourselves needs truth to prove it wrong. We can find a source of truth to combat those lies through what God says about us. I am a daughter of God who deserves great things, so I took my negative beliefs and stated the opposite—the truth. My negative belief that I wasn't worth it was transformed into I am worth it. I made a list of truths that proved the lies I believed to be false. When a negative emotion and thought came up, I had a list of truths to combat them, which helped me pursue my calling to start my coaching business.

For example, when I had a negative emotion and investigated that emotion, I was hit with a lie, or a negative core belief, such as I'm not worthy. When I knew that was not true, I turned that negative belief into a positive one, and I stated that I am worthy. In order for my brain to accept that new core belief, I had to prove it to myself. To do that, I listed out 5 things that proved that I was worthy. For example, my family loves me, I'm a daughter of God and He loves me, I am successful in my endeavors, everything always works out for me, and I have a husband that loves and believes in me.

Learning to transform our negative core beliefs into positive, truthful beliefs that will empower us to pursue our passions, desires, and calling is not a quick process. I take my clients through a four-week exercise to work through their negative emotions, learn how to capture their thoughts, and determine what their negative core beliefs are. It begins with being aware of negative feelings and writing down what you were thinking immediately before you had them. When you capture the thought you had before the emotion, you can assess the thoughts and trace them to a deeper level and determine your negative core belief, which might be a self-worth issue like it was for me. Challenge your thoughts, boil them down until you realize what their root is, and prove the negative core beliefs wrong with your actual truth.

…

# Journal, Sketch, Brainstorm

CHAPTER FOUR: PROVE IT! (SHOW ME)

# Chapter Five

## MAKE THE VISION - MAKE IT REAL

# Chapter Five

## MAKE THE VISION - MAKE IT REAL

As I mentioned in chapter one, my abilities as a coach are backed up by more than just education. I've gone through trying periods in my life that shaped and enabled me to help others. Difficult times can either weaken you or make you stronger. One such time in my life, though it was painful, made me stronger and equipped me with tools. Those tools helped me gain clarity and vision that pulled me through the chaos and got me to where I wanted to be.

In 2002, I gave birth to my daughter, Delaney, "Laney". She was born with a rare skin disease called Generalized Atrophic Benign Epidermolysis Bullosa which prevented her skin from being held onto her body. Her body lacked a protein that is meant to hold our skin on our body. When she was born, she was screaming in pain. I could tell there was something wrong from the way she was screaming, but it wasn't until she was handed to me that I knew something was very wrong. She cried in pain from being touched as I held her, and as she clenched at her blanket, I watched her fingernails pop off. I was confused and scared, and the doctor and nurses didn't know what was wrong with her. It was an extremely chaotic situation. Instead of celebrating my daughter entering the world, our lives were thrown into chaos.

After the delivery, I had to wait eight weeks for a diagnosis. Those were extremely difficult weeks, as I didn't know what was wrong with my daughter, or, more importantly, how to care for her. When we received the EB diagnosis, I was told that only a handful of people in the U.S. had the same form of the condition that she had. Even though we received a diagnosis, I didn't know what to do next. I had to take care of my daughter, but I had to figure out how to take care of a baby that couldn't be touched without experiencing immense pain. I was living in chaos and without a clue how take care of our fragile little baby. When you're in a situation like that, where your world has been turned upside down, you don't have a choice. You have to find a way to make it. In our case, we had to find a way to take care of Delaney, so we just did the best we could. We didn't have an option. It's what we had to do.

We learned through trial and error, right along with the doctors, how to take care of Laney. It was a day-by-day process, but we learned how to help her. We had to give her bleach baths, rub ointment on her wounds, and handle her gingerly so that we wouldn't injure her further. We also had to keep her safe from infection, since she was more susceptible because of her wounds. Everything around her could potentially cause an infection, so caring for her became a life or death struggle. Fortunately, I had help from family, medical professionals, and the hospital staff, even though they were learning how to take care of Laney right along with us.

Initially, the team at the hospital that helped me with Laney had numerous staff who would come and go. Since her disease was so rare, there wasn't a standard operating procedure they could easily follow. I worked with the hospital to come up with a way to take care of Laney, which began with downsizing the team that helped me with her. Since she needed to be protected from infection, we limited the amount of people who cared for her. We formed a specialized team that was knowledgeable about how to handle and treat her. It was important to have doctors and nurses who knew how to care for her, because bringing on new people meant training them, and training them meant Laney would experience more pain from their inexperience.

We had to think outside the box on how to take care of Laney. How do you care for a baby that doesn't have any skin? We had to rethink how to change her diaper without hurting her. Changing her diaper was especially challenging, because we had to figure out how to lift up her ankles when they didn't have any skin on them. We did our best for her, but there was only so much we could do, because her disease was so harmful.

Laney lived in excruciating pain every second of her life. Whenever there was friction against her skin, her skin would blister and eventually come off. There were wounds all over her body. Her nostrils were scarred shut. She had an eye infection caused by her blinking and scratching her cornea. There were blisters inside her throat that made eating and breathing extremely painful. Her esophagus was so scarred that she would never have a voice. Due to complications from her disease, she passed away when she was eight months old.

The funeral was at St. Lambert's, and it was so full, there were people out the door. I called the news when she was born, because I knew her story would have an impact. Over the course of her life, the news shared her story regularly, and Laney gained a following of people who were touched by her life. Many of them showed up at her funeral. When I gave her eulogy, I wanted to make an impression that she wasn't just a baby in pain with a rare skin disease. I said that even though she was in an immense amount of pain every moment of her life, she learned how to smile and blow raspberries through her blistered lips. I told the crowd that my daughter learned how to smile through pain every second of her life. Then I asked them, what's your excuse? I knew Laney's life had a purpose. I knew God was going to use her to impact people, so I wanted to use her story for a greater purpose.

After she passed away, the chaos wasn't over. I had gone through a painful whirlwind in my life, and I needed something to help me find peace. I needed to stop and relax, so I would repeat the mantra "Be still and know that I am God" over and over again. I've used that same mantra at other times in my life, like when I started my coaching business. It reminds me to stop and listen to God. When I was dealing with Laney's disease and then her death, I repeated that mantra to be reminded that God had control of my situation, so I could stop and give things to Him and everything would be OK. That helped me get through the crazy, and it gave me permission to hang things up sometimes and leave them in God's hands. Finding peace in the chaos made me able to move forward, but I also needed a path to move forward on. I found it by envisioning what I wanted my future to look like.

One day, my life was especially chaotic because I had homework and deadlines for school, and my kids were screaming for my attention, so I slowed down and repeated my mantra. Then I saw something on the television about envisioning a day in your life years from now. I started to think about what I wanted my life to look like in the future, so I started to write down what I wanted. I wanted to turn my negative, chaotic situation into something positive. I envisioned my life in the future, and I used that vision to guide me to what I wanted. It became the path I followed forward, from a place of chaos to clarity and fulfillment.

When you have a vision of what you want in the future, it can shape you toward your ultimate goal. If you have a vision, you know where you're going, so it's important to envision what you want in the future. Writing down your vision will help you remember it. Remind yourself of your vision daily, because it will motivate you to continue reaching toward the future and achieving what you want.

Another helpful way to envision your future is to create a vision board. A vision board is a more visual representation of what you want your life to be. It will help you capture the images and words of what you want your life to be like. Use your vision board as motivation to be constantly working toward what you want. Along with your written vision statement, a vision board will help you take steps to your ultimate goal.

When I was striving to move forward from my chaotic and painful situation, I envisioned what I wanted my life to be like in the future. My vision guided me forward and informed every step I took. I knew I wanted to help other people who were going through similar circumstances, just as I did with Laney. And I knew in the future I wanted to help coach. As I was creating my coaching business, my coach told me to look into the future and describe what it looked like. I wrote a story, describing a day in my life five years in the future. I wrote my story hour-by-hour, describing what I was doing. I made my husband breakfast and kissed him goodbye, drove my dream car to work, pulled up to my big, glass office building, walked inside and greeted my team of five people, signed some of my books, and then I left work to go to my book signing party. There was a line of people at my event, and I was picked up by a limo with my husband and friends, and then we went to dinner. My vision was very detailed, because I wanted to have a clear picture to strive for.

When I created my vision, I was claiming what was mine for the future. I was in a place of chaos, but I wanted success and happiness. I wanted to go from chaos to clarity and fulfillment. By envisioning my future, I was able to move forward and grow. You can do the same, but to effectively pursue your future, you need a vital piece of knowledge—your purpose.

# JOURNAL, SKETCH, BRAINSTORM

CHAPTER FIVE: MAKE THE VISION - MAKE IT REAL

CHAPTER FIVE: MAKE THE VISION - MAKE IT REAL

CHAPTER FIVE: MAKE THE VISION - MAKE IT REAL

# Chapter Six

## YOUR LIFE PURPOSE

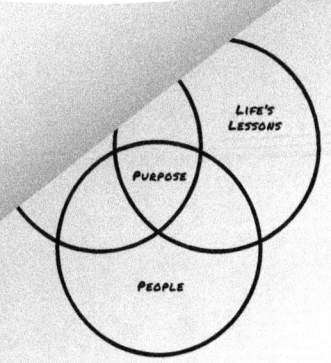

# Chapter Six

## YOUR LIFE PURPOSE

Ever since I was a little girl, I've known I was born to be a teacher. I've always felt fulfilled by teaching, so I knew that was a God-given gift. I knew I was meant to be a leader and help people. I wasn't the oldest kid in my family, but I took on that role. I used to walk my sisters home from school, make sure everyone was doing their homework, and I would get dinner ready for when my parents got home. Even though I grew up knowing what I was gifted at, I didn't know what I was supposed to do with my gifts until I knew my life's purpose.

I realized my purpose when I was a junior in high school. I was very close with my guidance counselor, and one day he came up to me and asked if I would speak to a group of women. He offered to give me extra credit for my speech class, so I agreed to speak to the group. I didn't do any prep work for my speech, I just told them the story of what I did the day before. I walked them through my busy day, telling them about getting up for school, taking my son to daycare, going to work, picking up my son and getting home late, and dealing with my boyfriend who was upset and physical with me. I wanted to show them how busy and chaotic my life was, with the hope they'd reevaluate their circumstances. I ended my talk by saying to them, if I can go to school and get an education to better my life, what's your excuse? When I was finished speaking to that group of women, I didn't really consider whether my talk helped them or not. Two years later, though, my mom told me she had a voicemail from a lady who heard me speak that day. She was empowered by my story, and it had changed her life.

When I found out my speech impacted one of the women in the group, I realized my life's purpose. I knew I was supposed to help people, which lined up perfectly with my God-given abilities. I had gifts that I was born with, and, as a teen mom, I had experienced some hard stuff that gave me lessons to pass on to others. It wasn't until I went through the painful experience with Laney, though, that I had an even clearer understanding of how to follow my life's purpose. I looked at the gifts I was born with, the lessons I learned from my experiences, and I decided to find a way to share them with others in the most purposeful way possible.

When Laney passed away, I had an understanding that there was a clear reason for her life. I knew God had a plan for her life, and, even through her death, he was fulfilling that plan. I also knew God had a purpose for me with Laney's story. I began to write down everything I learned from her life. I learned about wounds, handling my emotions in a healthy way, and I realized I didn't want anyone else to go through what I experienced.

Just a few days after Laney's funeral, I made a business plan about how I could help other families who were going through something similar. I decided to start a nonprofit called Laney Bear Care, to help families who had children with rare diseases. As I was starting the nonprofit, I was invited to the Sioux Falls Area Community Foundation, and I explained my idea and what I had gone through to thirteen business leaders in the Sioux Falls area. I told them I wanted to help families, and I received strong support from them. With their help, Laney Bear Care was formed, and some of the thirteen business leaders became board members of the nonprofit.

Laney Bear Care gave me purpose for the next year and a half as I helped nineteen families. I did anything I could to make their lives better, such as going to the hospital to stay with the child if the parents needed some free time. My main goal was to build them up, make them more able to care for their children, and empower them to raise the quality of their lives. Laney Bear Care gave my life purpose, but my life was not without challenges.

My son was ten years old at that time. As a single mom taking care of a nonprofit that didn't have enough money, I was barely making ends meet. After a year and a half, I couldn't maintain my role without stretching myself too thin. I met with my board and told them I wasn't able to make the nonprofit work financially. I also told them I felt guilty I wasn't able to serve the families anymore. It was unsustainable, but it wasn't a failure. Nineteen families were helped by Laney Bear Care. I was able to use my life's purpose to take those families by the hand and help them. I was there for them to help them not feel alone. And I was able to help them get resources that improved their lives. Most importantly, though, the lives of other families were improved, because we saw the gaps from our journey with Laney, and we did something about it.

Although it was painful and chaotic, God used my experience with Laney for a greater purpose. Her life was part of a greater plan that helped many families get help for their children. I discovered my life's purpose through Laney's life. She showed me what to do with my abilities and passion. Through Laney Bear Care, I pursued my purpose and began coaching people by walking with them through life. I drew lessons from the hardest experience of my life and used them to catapult me forward and serve my purpose.

A lot of other coaches place an importance on finding your purpose, but they advise you to find purpose from what makes you most happy. I begin by asking you about the hardest experiences of your life. From those experiences, I help you draw out the lessons you've learned, how you've grown, and how you can use that to your advantage. I also help you connect the lessons you've learned to your God-given abilities. Often times, the lessons we learn during hard times strengthen the abilities we were born with. Through examining the challenging, formative times in your life, and your gifts and lessons, you can find your life's purpose and be catapulted into a future that is fulfilling, rewarding, and successful.

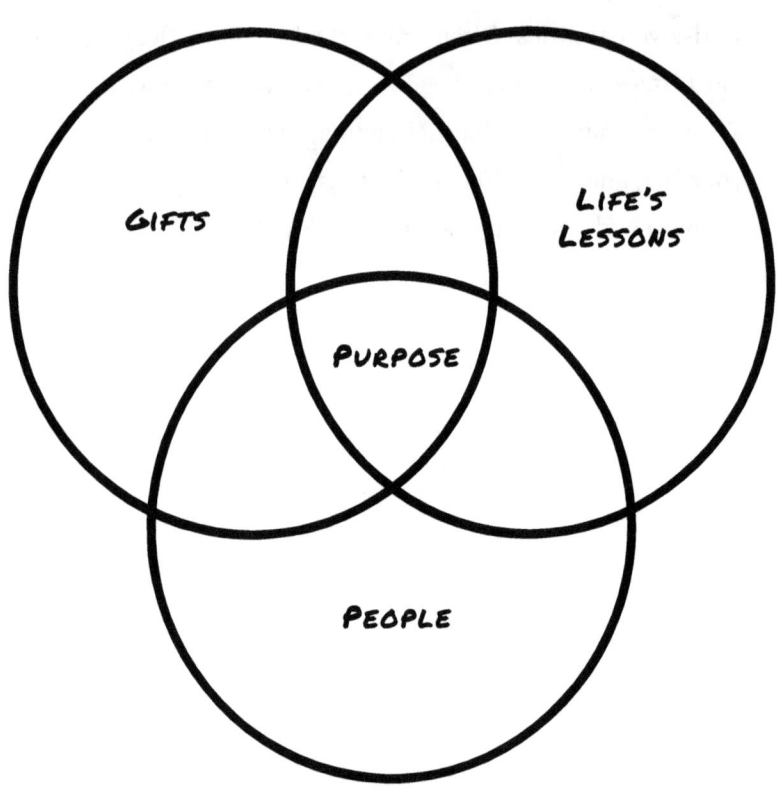

# JOURNAL, SKETCH, BRAINSTORM

# Chapter Seven

## YOUR CHOICE

# Chapter Seven

## YOUR CHOICE

In order to pursue your purpose and make any progressive change in your life, you have to choose it. How do you want your life to be? Do you want it to be transformed and catapulted into fulfillment and success? Finding success and living a more fulfilled life begins with choosing to make a change. Transformation begins with choosing to make changes to your life that will catapult you forward. You have to continually choose transformation, progress, and success. If you're happy and comfortable, you can stay there and enjoy it. If not, it's time to make a change in your life, which begins with realizing what your version of success and happiness is.

Choosing transformation is about choosing happiness. We always want what we don't have, because we feel like we're going to be happier once we have that thing. For example, we want to exercise because we think being healthy and looking good will make us happier. Or we want to have better communication skills with our employees so that we're considered good bosses, which will make us happier. Happiness matters, so it's important to realize what happiness means in your life. When you know what your happiness is, you'll have a clearer understanding of what your end goal of transformation is, which will free you to be catapulted toward your target. When you're happy, you're more likely to achieve success, because your happiness will inspire other people to be happy, which will enrich your life. People and opportunities will be drawn to you if you're happy, and you'll be affected in a positive manner that will expedite your journey to success.

Happiness is not the only key to success, though. In order to achieve success, you have to grow and be transformed. Just like happiness, transformation is a choice. It begins with using abilities you have and the tools outlined in this book.

Each of us is born with abilities, and, throughout life, we learn lessons that make us stronger. We need tools, though, that help us make the most out of the lessons we've learned. The tools in this book can catapult you toward your best life, but they're only a start. By using the tools outlined in this book, you're going to create a better life for yourself. It takes a daily choice to use them, though. Tools are pointless if you don't use them, so you have to be diligent about using them, as they will help you transform and grow toward success. As you grow, opportunities will open up to you and you'll begin to see change in your life.

Right now, you have a choice on how to live your life. If you're unhappy with your current circumstances, you can choose to change your life. You can choose happiness and transformation, and you can choose to pursue success. If you had an opportunity to live your best life, wouldn't you choose it? You have the opportunity to choose it every day, and you can make it happen by implementing the tools in this book into your life and pursuing growth and transformation. If you do so, your life will change dramatically, and you'll be catapulted toward success.

You have a choice on how to live your life and you can change it. You can choose happiness regardless of the situation you're in.

If you change nothing, you will remain the same. If you're happy with that, you wouldn't still be reading this book. My hope for you is that you'll see your potential through reading this book, that you'll have a glimpse into the future of what your life can be like, and that you'll be encouraged and empowered to pursue your version of success. Finding success begins with assessing your life. Look at your life. What gifts have you always had? What lessons have you learned? What are you going to do with your experiences and abilities? How are you going to live out your purpose?

I hope this book helps you dig deeper into your life and find your purpose. My goal for you is to live a transformed life, free from the weight of your past experiences holding you back. The challenges we face in life don't have to hold us down like boulders. I want to help you shed whatever is holding you back from living your best life. The tools in this book will help you grow, but if you want to go deeper and really pursue your purpose and find success in your life, reach out to me and I'll help you catapult your life forward.

# Journal, Sketch, Brainstorm

CHAPTER SEVEN: YOUR CHOICE

# CHAPTER SEVEN: YOUR CHOICE

# About the Author

# About the Author

Tanya Unterbrunner is the founder and Lead Coach at Catapult Coaching and Consulting. Tanya created True Life Advisor in 2012 and re-branded this business to Catapult Coaching and Consulting after seeing the phenomenal success of her clients. Her passion is to help people discover how to let their lessons of the past CATAPULT them into living the life they deserve, instead of it being a reason for them to be stuck in their past.

Tanya knows first-hand about the struggles of letting life get the best of us instead of us getting the best of life. She was a teen mom who survived an abusive relationship while attending high school and working two jobs. She catapulted in her life after her eight-month-old daughter passed away from a rare skin disease and she chose to start a non-profit organization to help others going through similar circumstances. She now lives her best life with her soul-mate as they raise their three children in Sioux Falls, SD, while growing her business to help others do the same.

**Tanya Unterbrunner**

Founder and Lead Coach, Catapult Coaching and Consulting

**Website:**

CatapultMyLife.com

**Phone:**

605-681-NEWU (6398)

**Email:**

Team@CatapultMyLife.com

**Facebook:**

Tanya L. Unterbrunner

ABOUT THE AUTHOR

# About the Company

# About the Company

## Catapult

Catapult Coaching and Consulting is a practice located in Sioux Falls, SD. The company was originally founded in 2012 by Tanya Unterbrunner and was named True Life Advisor. The growth and the clarity brought on by the clients led to the rebranding in 2018. The main focus of the business has always been to help people live their best life.

There are many types of coaching in the world, and Tanya felt a calling to stay in the space of a life coach. Knowing that the coach should specialize in a certain area, when True Life Advisor began, Tanya could say what she specialized in most was life. As time went on and Tanya saw hundreds of clients, the time that she was most excited for her clients was when they realized that they could use their past to launch them into their future without allowing it to hold them back. When Tanya's clients could shift their perspective on their current circumstances and their future, she knew they were forever transformed. That was the birth of Catapult Coaching and Consulting.

Catapult Coaching is unlike other coaching. It truly has a unique style that focuses on the entire individual, and really targets a key area that, when changed or uncovered, will catapult the individual into the best version of themselves. When this is accomplished, they will be able to conquer goals and challenges alike.

**Tanya Unterbrunner**
Founder and Lead Coach, Catapult Coaching and Consulting

**Website:**
CatapultMyLife.com

**Phone:**
605-681-NEWU (6398)

**Email:**
Team@CatapultMyLife.com

**Facebook:**
@CatapultMyLife

www.ingramcontent.com/pod-product-compliance
Lightning Source LLC
LaVergne TN
LVHW051836080426
835512LV00018B/2906